FOSSILS

by Jenny Fretland VanVoorst

Content Consultant
Dr. Kevin Theissen
Associate Professor and Chair
Department of Geology
University of Saint Thomas

Core Library

An Imprint of Abdo Publishing
www.abdopublishing.com

www.abdopublishing.com

Published by Abdo Publishing, a division of ABDO, PO Box 398166, Minneapolis, Minnesota 55439. Copyright © 2015 by Abdo Consulting Group, Inc. International copyrights reserved in all countries. No part of this book may be reproduced in any form without written permission from the publisher. Core Library™ is a trademark and logo of Abdo Publishing.

Printed in the United States of America, North Mankato, Minnesota
042014
092014

THIS BOOK CONTAINS
RECYCLED MATERIALS

Cover Photo: iStockphoto/Thinkstock
Interior Photos: iStockphoto/Thinkstock, 1, 19, 28, 38 (top), 38 (middle), 42; Ethan Miller/Getty Images/Thinkstock, 4; Mark Higgins/Shutterstock Images, 7, 45; Shutterstock Images, 9, 15, 17, 39; AP Images, 10; Zoonar RF/Thinkstock, 12; Mike Saunders/Dorling Kindersley, 20; Marcel Clemens/ Shutterstock Images, 22; dpa/picture-alliance/AP Images, 25; Science Photo Library/SuperStock, 26; Natursports/Shutterstock Images, 30; Getty Images/Thinkstock, 33; Euan Denholm/Reuters/Corbis, 34; Jana Shea/Thinkstock, 37; Chris Hellier/Corbis, 38 (bottom); Andrei Orlov/ Shutterstock Images, 43

Editor: Lauren Coss
Series Designer: Becky Daum

Library of Congress Control Number: 2014932345

Cataloging-in-Publication Data
VanVoorst, Jenny Fretland.
  Fossils / Jenny Fretland VanVoorst.
    p. cm. -- (Rocks and minerals)
Includes bibliographical references and index.
ISBN 978-1-62403-385-8
1. Fossils--Juvenile literature. 2. Paleontology--Juvenile literature.   I. Title.
560--dc23

2014932345

CONTENTS

CHAPTER ONE
What Are Fossils? **4**

CHAPTER TWO
How Do Fossils Form? **12**

CHAPTER THREE
Other Types of Fossils **22**

CHAPTER FOUR
Learning from the Past **30**

In the Field 42

Stop and Think 44

Glossary 46

Learn More 47

Index 48

About the Author .48

WHAT ARE FOSSILS?

Have you ever picked up a strange-looking rock at the park or beach? It may have had the shape of a small fish or plant on it. Or perhaps you've seen a skeleton of a dinosaur on display at a museum. The rock and the skeleton have something very important in common. They are both fossils.

This Tyrannosaurus rex fossil came from a dinosaur that lived more than 66 million years ago.

Fossilized Bacteria

The oldest fossils are actually fossils of tiny bacteria. Bacteria are tiny living things that are made of a single cell. Fossilized bacteria have been found in western Australia. They are believed to be 3.5 billion years old. The fossils were found in a pattern. This means that even the earliest life had some form of organization to it. Scientists believe the bacteria may have operated as a colony, with different kinds of bacteria doing different tasks. But these bacteria may tell us about more than just life on Earth. Understanding our planet's earliest life forms may help guide scientists who are searching for life on other planets!

Many Different Fossils

Fossils are the preserved remains of ancient living things. They are made of plants, animals, and other creatures that died long ago and have been preserved in rock. Under the right conditions, just about any living thing you can think of could become a fossil. Fossils can come from stems, leaves, bones, teeth, shells, animal tracks, and even animal droppings. And because

These fossilized dinosaur tracks near Tuba City, Arizona, were probably formed by a dinosaur called the Dilophosaurus.

fossils are made of rock, they can be found anywhere that rocks are found.

Fossils can be found in all shapes and sizes. There are fossils from the sea and from the land. There are fossils of insects, and plants, and dinosaurs. There are fossils in tar and fossils in stone. All these fossils were once living things. After death, natural processes preserved their remains.

Clues to the Past

Fossils tell the story of Earth's past. But they are an important part of our present as well. Scientists can study fossils to learn what the planet was like millions and billions of years ago. Fossils can tell us about the plants and animals that once roamed our planet. They also offer clues about how climate and geography have changed. For example, whale fossils have been found high in the Andes Mountains of South America. The fossils, which once rested on the bottom of the ocean, are now at 5,000 feet (1,524 m) above sea level. This tells us that over millions of years, the mountains rose up in an area that was once the sea floor.

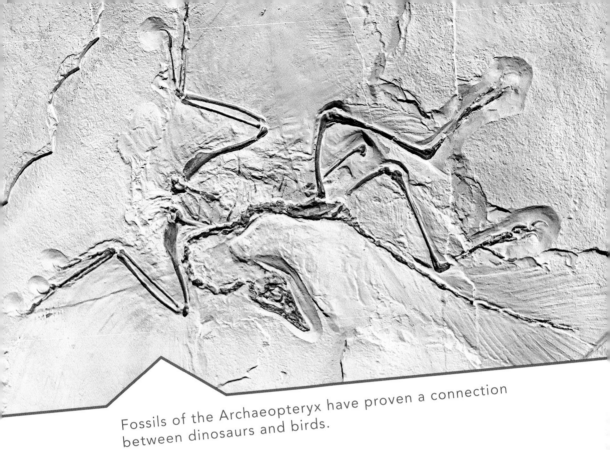

Fossils of the Archaeopteryx have proven a connection between dinosaurs and birds.

Fossils also help us learn about life on Earth today. They show us how life has evolved over billions of years. Many fossils have living relatives.
For example, by studying fossils, we have learned that today's birds are actually related to the dinosaurs of long ago. A fossilized Archaeopteryx skeleton found in 1861 provided the link. It was obviously the skeleton of a reptile, but it was clear that the living animal had had feathers.

In the 1920s, geologist and paleontologist Henry Fairfield Osborn argued that fossils could be used to prove that plants and animals had evolved over time.

A plant or dinosaur doesn't turn to stone overnight. It takes millions of years for a fossil to form. The fossils you find at the park or on the beach are the remains of plants or creatures that lived on Earth long before humans. How can a fish that swam in the sea 4 million years ago appear on a rock you hold in your hand? To understand how a fossil forms, we first need to look at how the planet is made.

In 1925 a court case known as the Scopes Trial challenged the teaching of evolution in the schools. Geologist and paleontologist Henry Fairfield Osborn wrote a book in response to the Scopes Trial. Osborn argued that the fossil record supported evolution:

> The earth speaks not of a succession of distinct creations but of a continuous ascent, in which, as the millions of years roll by, increasing perfection of structure and beauty of form are found; out of the water-breathing fish arises the air-breathing amphibian; out of the land-living amphibian arises the land-living, air-breathing reptile, these two kinds of creeping things resembling each other closely. The earth speaks loudly and clearly of the ascent of the bird from one kind of reptile and of the mammal from another kind of reptile.
>
> Source: Henry Fairfield Osborn. *The Earth Speaks to Bryan.* New York: Scribner's, 1925. Print. 5–6.

Consider Your Audience

Review this passage closely. How would you adapt it for a different audience, such as your parents, your principal, or younger friends? Write a blog post, relating this same information for the new audience. How does your new approach differ from the original text and why?

CHAPTER TWO

HOW DO FOSSILS FORM?

Earth is made up of four layers. The crust is the outside layer. It is the thinnest layer, and it forms Earth's surface. The crust is made up of rock, and it is completely solid. It's where we stand and walk and play. It's where fossils are formed and found. Oceans cover much of Earth's crust.

Just below the crust is a layer called the mantle. Like the crust, the mantle is made of rock. But in

These stromatolites in Australia are the fossilized remains of ancient bacteria.

Earth on the Move

Our planet is constantly changing. The earth is shifting under our feet, but it happens so slowly we can't feel it. Earth's continents are part of moving pieces of the crust called plates. Sometimes these plates crash together. Sometimes they pull apart. This motion shifts layers of rock, moving older layers to the surface and pushing newer rocks below. Over millions of years, plates can move rocks from one part of the world to another. They can deposit rock from the ocean floor on the top of a mountain. Because of this, fossilized animals or plants may not have necessarily lived where they were found.

the mantle, the rock is under so much heat and pressure that it can stretch like hot tar on a road. Sometimes magma, or fully melted rock, rises up through the mantle. If it breaks through to the surface, a volcano can form.

Below the mantle is the earth's core. The core is divided into two layers: the outer core and the inner core. The outer core is metal. It is so hot that the metal is melted into liquid. The inner core is also made of metal. The inner core is

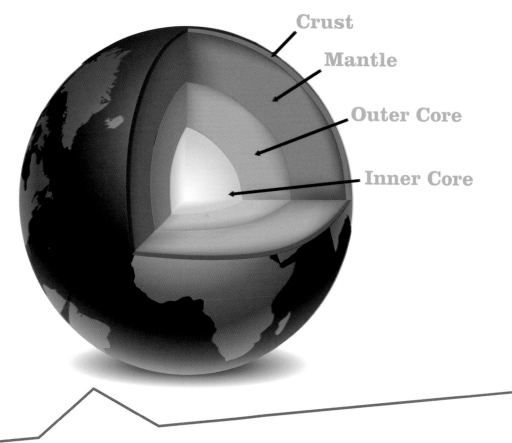

Crust

Mantle

Outer Core

Inner Core

Earth's layers

also very hot, but the pressure of everything above it pressing down is so great that it remains solid. No one has traveled past the crust. Scientists learn about the earth's interior using seismometers. These instruments measure activity deep inside the earth.

Earth has three kinds of rocks: igneous, sedimentary, and metamorphic. Igneous rocks begin as melted rock, or magma, deep inside the earth.

15

They often form when the magma cools into solid rock either at or below Earth's surface. Metamorphic rocks begin as either igneous, sedimentary, or other metamorphic rocks. They transform into new kinds of rocks when exposed to great heat or pressure.

Sedimentary rocks are made of sediment. Sediment consists of mud, clay, silt, or sand. Over time, the sediment settles and hardens into layers. New layers of sediment settle on top of old ones. The weight of the layers compacts and hardens the sediment below. It becomes rock. It takes millions of years for sedimentary rock to form.

The Grand Canyon

Have you ever been to the Grand Canyon? If so, you probably noticed the horizontal stripes along the canyon walls. Each stripe is a slightly different color from the one next to it. The stripes are different layers of sedimentary rock. The youngest rocks are at the top of the canyon. The older layers are at the canyon's bottom. This makes walking down into the canyon a little like walking back in time.

The layers of sedimentary rock in the Grand Canyon can be used to tell how old different parts of the canyon are.

Eventually, layers of sedimentary rock build up and up and up.

Buried in Stone

Most fossils are found in sedimentary rock. They are formed when a living thing dies. But the likelihood of any one dead organism becoming a fossil is very small. A series of very specific events needs to happen.

First, the organism's body must be kept away from scavengers. It must also be sheltered from wind, rain, or snow. Then, a layer of sediment must cover the body before it has begun to break down. The ocean floor is an ideal place for this to happen. That's why so many fossils are of sea creatures that lived long ago.

Eventually, the skeleton is surrounded by rock. The soft parts of the body have rotted away. Finally, even the skeleton decomposes. This leaves a hole in the rock in the shape of the animal's skeleton. Geologists call this hole a mold.

You may have seen molds of prehistoric creatures such as ammonites and trilobites in museums. These organisms are commonly found as mold fossils. Animal tracks are mold fossils as well. They form when an animal steps in mud or soft clay. The mud or clay hardens around the tracks before the next layer of sediment has settled. When the next layer forms, it sits atop the impression rather than mixing with it.

Trilobites, such as the one preserved in this fossil, were a group of marine animals that lived 500 million years ago.

A mold fossil is a two-dimensional impression of an organism. But sometimes fossilization continues past the mold stage. These fossils are in 3-D. Such fossils occur when water enters the newly created mold. The water leaves mineral deposits behind. The minerals collect and fill the hole, creating a cast of the skeleton. This is the way those spectacular dinosaur

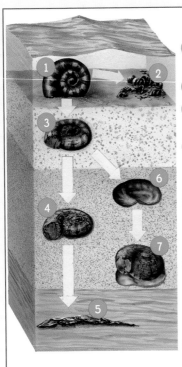

1. An ammonite dies and sinks to the bottom of the ocean.

2. The soft parts of the body decay.

3. New layers of sediment settle on the hard ammonite shell.

4. The shell slowly breaks down; its organic parts are replaced with minerals from the water. Eventually, the shell becomes stone.

5. Over millions of years, the seabed the ammonite was buried in is compressed into rock. Eventually, the ocean recedes, and the rock above the ammonite erodes away.

6. Sometimes rock forms around the ammonite shell, but the shell erodes before it can become fossilized. When this happens, only the imprint of the shell will remain.

7. When the seabed erodes away, the imprint can be seen.

Fossilization

This diagram shows the process of fossilization. How does the information presented above compare with what you have learned from the description of fossilization in this book? How is the diagram similar to what you have learned? Does it provide additional information that the text does not?

bones you see in museums were formed. They are naturally made reproductions of living dinosaur bones.

Earthquakes, landslides, or the gradual shifting of the earth's crust bring the rock that surrounds the cast to the surface. Wind and rain wear away the stone in a process called erosion. Erosion exposes the fossil.

Many things can become fossils. Some fossils show the delicate imprint of a leaf. Others preserve the firm footprints of a prehistoric cat. There are fossilized tree stumps and giant stone shark teeth. All of these fossils are the remains of something that was once alive. They give us a glimpse of life on Earth millions of years ago.

FURTHER EVIDENCE

Chapter Two explains how once-living things become fossils. It also describes how the earth builds up and breaks down rock over time. If you could pick out one of the main points in this chapter, what would it be? What evidence is given to support that point? Visit the website below to learn more about the process of fossilization. Then choose a quote from the website that relates to this chapter. Does this quote support a main point in Chapter Two? Does it make a new point? Write a few sentences explaining how the quote you found relates to this chapter.

Fossils
www.mycorelibrary.com/fossils

OTHER TYPES OF FOSSILS

Most fossils are found in sedimentary rock. They are formed when organisms leave impressions in stone or become stone themselves. But there are many different ways to make a fossil. Some fossils don't become rocks at all! Nature has other ways to preserve the remains of living things.

The soft parts of this fish decomposed, leaving a hard skeleton that was fossilized.

Dinosaur Eggs

Dinosaur eggs, like all fossils, are rare. But dinosaur eggs with fossilized dinosaur embryos inside are even more rare! Because they are so rare, scientists must be careful when trying to find out what's inside a dinosaur egg. Sometimes they X-ray the egg. Sometimes they dissolve the shell in acid. If they're lucky, they'll find an embryo, or developing dinosaur, inside. By studying fossilized embryos, scientists learn how dinosaurs developed inside the egg.

Mummies

Some preserved remains are called fossils even though they have not become stone. You've probably learned about mummies made by ancient Egyptians. Nature can make mummies too. Frozen organisms have been found preserved as mummies. Freezing allows the soft body parts of an animal, such as skin, hair, and organs, to be preserved. The frigid temperatures slow the rate at which the body breaks down. A thick layer of ice or frozen soil protects the body from scavengers and the environment. Long-extinct mammoths have been discovered frozen

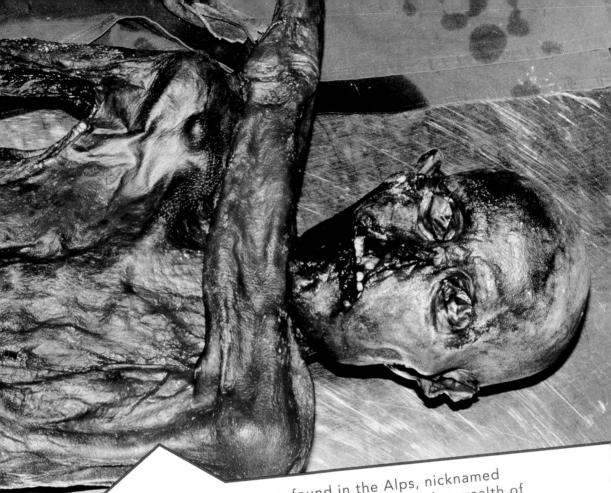

The mummy of the man found in the Alps, nicknamed Ötzi the Iceman, has provided scientists with a wealth of information about what life was like 5,000 years ago.

in glacial ice. Some still had fur and blood. The 5,000-year-old body of a man was found mummified in ice in the Alps on the border of Italy and Austria. He was so well preserved that scientists were able to study the contents of his stomach. They could even figure out what he ate for his last meal!

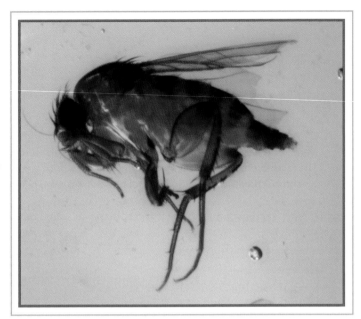

Insects fossilized in amber are so well preserved that even wings, legs, and hairs are visible.

Freezing can preserve remains well, but hot and dry conditions can also halt decomposition. The hot, dry air sucks moisture from the body. Tissues become dry and tough like beef jerky. Fossils found in hot, dry conditions are a natural version of the mummies of ancient Egypt.

Amber

Other fossils can be even more perfectly preserved than mummies. Have you ever seen a clear glass paperweight with a spider or bug inside? Similar things can be found in nature.

Insects, spiders, and even small lizards and frogs have been found millions of years after they lived and died. A number of events must occur for a creature to be preserved in amber. First the animal stepped in tree resin. The creature became trapped and died. Over time the resin changed to a hard, clear material called amber. The organisms inside the amber were protected from decomposition. Hair, wings, and other soft parts were preserved.

Tar

Tar is another naturally occurring sticky matter that can preserve bodies. In some places, underground tar leaks to the surface and forms huge lakes or pits.

La Brea Tar Pits

The La Brea Tar Pits in Los Angeles, California, are famous for their collection of fossilized mammals and plants. More than 135 species of birds and nearly 60 species of mammals have been found in the tar pits. Some of these animals, such as camels, mammoths, and saber-toothed tigers, are extinct or no longer found in North America. The bones that remain have absorbed the oil from the tar and become a dark brown color.

A display at the La Brea Tar Pits shows how mammoths may have gotten trapped in the tar thousands of years ago.

Like the insects in amber, the animals got stuck in the tar. It preserved their skeletons.

Fossils can form in many ways in a variety of places. But whether they are found in rock or ice, amber or tar, all fossils have something to teach us. By studying fossils we can learn about the creatures and plants of the distant past. We can also discover how they grew, what they ate, and how they interacted. Fossils help us understand how life evolved on Earth. Fossils also help us learn about past climates. They provide evidence for ice ages and periods that were warmer and wetter than our climate today.

EXPLORE ONLINE

Chapter Three focuses on how scientists can use fossils to learn about the planet's history. It also touches on the La Brea Tar Pits. As you know, every source is different. How is the information given in the website about the tar pits different from the information in this chapter? What information is the same? What can you learn from this website?

La Brea Tar Pits
www.mycorelibrary.com/fossils

CHAPTER FOUR

LEARNING FROM THE PAST

Scientists who study fossils are called paleontologists. Fossils help them see into the past and learn about species that lived long ago. Paleontologists have even used fossils to estimate the point at which life on Earth began—3.8 to 3.5 billion years ago.

A big part of a scientist's job is to ask a lot of questions. Paleontologists ask questions about what

Paleontologists in Spain dig for fossils of ancient humans.

early life on Earth was like. They want to know how living things have changed over time. They also want to understand what today's plants and animals have in common with plants and animals of long ago.

The Fossil Record

Paleontologists look to the fossil record for answers to many of these questions. The fossil record is the collection of all known fossils and the information learned from them. The fossil record provides information that helps scientists identify and understand new discoveries. It begins with the earliest known fossils from 3.5 billion years ago. The oldest fossil ever found was a type of algae.

By comparing the oldest fossils with more recent ones, we can learn

A Day for Fossils!

Did you know there's a special holiday dedicated to fossils? National Fossil Day is a yearly celebration organized by the US National Park Service. This day was created in 2010 to draw attention to fossils, protect them, and promote a greater appreciation of their scientific and educational value.

A researcher sorts tiny fossils found near the La Brea Tar Pits.

how animals and landscapes changed over time. For example, an area of land might contain many fossils of marine animals. This tells scientists that land may once have been covered in water. By studying the fossilized skeletons of human ancestors, scientists have learned how we've evolved. Over time, the height of our bodies and the size of our brains have been increasing.

This fossilized skull is from a child who lived more than 3 million years ago.

The fossil record helps scientists piece together an understanding of the world. But the fossil record is full of gaps. We don't have fossils for every plant or animal at every stage in its development. Many species died and decayed without ever leaving a fossil. But scientists use the knowledge that's been collected to make educated guesses. For example, rocks in a particular area may contain fossils scientists recognize from a certain time period. This means it is likely that fossils found in other rocks in the area are from the same time period. Ammonites, a prehistoric ancestor of the squid, are fossils often used to date other fossils. Because scientists know ammonites went extinct about 65 million years ago, they know that fossils found alongside ammonites are most likely at least 65 million years old. Ammonites are known as index fossils. They serve as an index to help place other fossils in time.

Layers of rock hold clues too. If fossils of several species are found in one layer of rock, it is likely that these species lived at the same time. Fossils in the layers below are likely older. Fossils in the layers above are probably newer. Scientists can look at layers of older or younger rock to learn how the organisms changed over time. By comparing dinosaur bones with the bones of modern birds, scientists discovered that the two animals are actually related.

Living Fossils

Have you ever heard of a living fossil? This is a plant or animal that looks very similar to its ancestors. It has changed so little over time that the modern plant or animal is like a living copy of the fossil. Scientist call these plants and animals living fossils. Ferns, gingko trees, horseshoe crabs, and coelacanth fish are all considered living fossils.

Eras of Earth

Fossils help scientists break up the long history of life on Earth into more manageable chunks. The divisions between these periods of time mark a major change in the fossil record. This is when certain fossils may have appeared or disappeared. You've probably heard of the Jurassic Period or

Horseshoe crabs have changed very little in the last 400 million years.

the Mesozoic Era. These divisions of time are useful shortcuts. They help scientists remember what Earth was like during that period. When scientists talk about the Mesozoic Era, for example, they know that mammals, birds, and flowering plants appeared for the first time. They know that Earth was hotter than it is today. They know that the Jurassic Period, in the middle of the Mesozoic Era, saw the rise of the dinosaurs.

Fossils of human beings appeared in the Quaternary Period, the third period of the

PALEOZOIC ERA 541 MILLION YEARS AGO TO 252.2 MILLION YEARS AGO	CAMBRIAN PERIOD	541 TO 485.4 MILLION YEARS AGO
	ORDOVICIAN PERIOD	485.4 TO 443.4 MILLION YEARS AGO
	SILURIAN PERIOD	443.4 TO 419.2 MILLION YEARS AGO
	DEVONIAN PERIOD	419.2 TO 358.9 MILLION YEARS AGO
Trilobite	CARBONIFEROUS PERIOD	358.9 TO 298.9 MILLION YEARS AGO
	PERMIAN PERIOD	298.9 TO 252.2 MILLION YEARS AGO
MESOZOIC ERA 252.2 MILLION YEARS AGO TO 66 MILLION YEARS AGO	TRIASSIC PERIOD	252.2 TO 201.3 MILLION YEARS AGO
	JURASSIC PERIOD	201.3 TO 145 MILLION YEARS AGO
Ammonite	CRETACEOUS PERIOD	145 TO 66 MILLION YEARS AGO
CENOZOIC ERA 66 MILLION YEARS AGO TO PRESENT	PALEOGENE PERIOD	66 TO 23 MILLION YEARS AGO
	NEOGENE PERIOD	23 MILLION TO 2.6 MILLION YEARS AGO
Bear	QUATERNARY PERIOD	2.6 MILLION YEARS AGO TO PRESENT

Fossils over Time

Study this diagram of geological time periods and the fossils that existed then. How does the information presented compare with what you have learned from the text? How is it similar to what you have learned? Does it provide additional information that the text does not? Does it leave out important facts that the text addresses?

Cenozoic Era. That's the period we live in right now.

But scientists have found fossils of human ancestors that are much older.

Maybe you'll find the next important clue to the past on your own fossil hunt.

Be a Fossil Hunter!

Fossils have been incredibly important to our understanding of life on Earth. But paleontologists can only study what they can find. Anyone can be a fossil hunter. You just need a good eye, plenty of patience, and a lot of luck. If you would like to be a fossil hunter, you need to know where to look.

Fossils are most often found in sedimentary rock. Limestone is a good place to start. This common sedimentary rock often contains fragments of coral and other marine skeletons. You're likely to find some nearby, no matter where you are.

Fossils can be both rare and difficult to find. It can be hard to tell which rocks have fossils in them and which just have strange markings. Paleontologists spend a lot of time looking at rocks without finding any fossils. Don't be discouraged if you don't find anything. But don't give up. Fossils help us learn about our past and understand our present. Maybe you will make the next big discovery!

Richard E. Leakey is a famous paleontologist. He is best known for his and his family's work excavating early human fossils in Africa. He described what it takes to be a good fossil hunter:

> A fossil hunter needs sharp eyes and a keen search image. . . . Yet even when one has a good internal radar, the search is incredibly more difficult than it sounds. Not only are fossils often the same color as the rocks among which they are found, so they blend in with the background; they are also usually broken into odd-shaped fragments. . . . In our business, we don't expect to find a whole skull lying on the surface staring up at us. The typical find is a small piece of petrified bone. The fossil hunter's search therefore has to have an infinite number of dimensions, matching every conceivable angle of every shape of fragment of every bone on the human body.

Source: Richard E. Leakey and Roger Lewin. Origins Reconsidered: In Search of What Makes Us Human. New York: Doubleday, 1992. Print. 26.

Back It Up

Leakey is using evidence to support a point. Write a paragraph describing the point he is making. Then write down two or three pieces of evidence Leakey uses to make the point.

How are the fossils you made similar to these fossilized shells?

Molds and Casts

Who wants to wait millions of years for a fossil? Make one yourself in less than an hour. First, flatten a ball of modeling clay into the bottom of a small paper cup. The clay should fill less than half the cup. Smooth out the clay so there are no lumps or bumps. Now choose some objects to fossilize. Shells, leaves, or plastic dinosaurs or bugs will work just fine. Press them into the clay and then remove them. Next, mix a small amount of plaster of paris in a bowl, following the directions on the package. Pour the plaster into your cup. Wait until the plaster is hard—about 30 minutes. Then tear away the paper cup to see your fossil!

Many fossils are found on beaches.

Fossil Hunting

The best place to find fossils is in sedimentary rock. Ask an adult to help you find a good place to start looking. Ask permission if you plan to hunt on someone else's property. Your best tools for fossil hunting are your eyes. Many fossils have been found lying in plain sight. A magnifying glass will give you an up-close look at the rocks you find. If you think you may have found something important—like something you might expect to see in a museum—it's best to find an expert to help. They'll want to study rocks in the area where the fossil was found.

Say What?

Studying fossils can mean learning a lot of new vocabulary. Find five words in this book that you've never heard before. Use a dictionary to find out what they mean. Then write the meanings in your own words, and use each word in a new sentence.

Tell the Tale

This book discusses the ways paleontologists search for fossils. Imagine you are a paleontologist planning a fossil hunt. Write a few paragraphs that tell about how you would plan your trip. What kind of fossil would you look for? How would you decide where to look? What would you bring with you? Be sure to set the scene, develop a sequence of events, and offer a conclusion.

Surprise Me

Chapter Two discusses methods of fossilization. Fossils can be interesting and surprising. After reading this book, what two or three facts stood out about these fossils? Write a few sentences about each fact. Why did you find them surprising?

You Are There

This book discusses the fields of geology and paleontology. Imagine you are a paleontologist studying the La Brea Tar Pits. Write a journal entry describing your research. What kind of fossils might you find there? How do these fossils provide clues to Earth's past?

GLOSSARY

cast
a fossil that forms inside a hollow space

decompose
to rot and fall apart

embryo
a human or animal in the early stages of development before it is born or hatched

geologist
a scientist who studies rocks, minerals, and fossils to learn about the earth

mineral
a solid substance that is not alive

mold
a hollow space that forms after bits of mud, sand, stone, or shell bury remains and the remains rot away

organism
an individual living thing

paleontologist
a scientist who collects and studies fossils

scavenger
an organism that typically feeds on dead animals

species
a group of animals or plants that are similar and can produce young animals or plants

LEARN MORE

Books

Peterson, Christine. *Fantastic Fossils*. Edina, MN: Abdo, 2010.

Taylor, Paul D. *Fossil*. New York: Dorling Kindersley, 2004.

Tomecek, Steve. *Everything Rocks and Minerals*. Washington, DC: National Geographic, 2010.

Websites

To learn more about Rocks and Minerals, visit **booklinks.abdopublishing.com**. These links are routinely monitored and updated to provide the most current information available.

Visit **www.mycorelibrary.com** for free additional tools for teachers and students.

INDEX

amber, 26–27, 28
ammonites, 18, 20, 35
animal tracks, 6, 18, 21
Archaeopteryx, 9

bacteria, 6

cast fossils, 19–20
climate, 8, 29

dinosaurs, 5, 7, 9–10,
 19–20, 24, 36, 37

Earth's eras, 36–38
Earth's layers, 13–15
 core, 14–15
 crust, 13, 14, 15, 20
 mantle, 13–14
erosion, 20
evolution, 9, 11, 29, 33

fossil fuels, 8

fossil hunting, 40, 41
fossil record, 11, 32–33,
 35–36
fossilization, 7, 17–20,
 21

Grand Canyon, 16

igneous rocks, 15–16
imprints, 20, 21
index fossils, 35–36
insects, 7, 27

La Brea Tar Pits, 27, 29
Leakey, Richard E., 41
living fossils, 36

magma, 14–16
metamorphic rocks,
 15–16
mold fossils, 18–19
mummies, 24–25

National Fossil Day, 32

Osborn, Henry Fairfield,
 11

paleontologists, 11, 31,
 32, 40, 41
plants, 5, 7, 8, 10, 14,
 27, 28, 32, 35, 36, 37
plates, 14

scientists, 6, 8, 15, 24,
 25, 29, 31, 32–33,
 35–38
Scopes Trial, 11
sedimentary rocks,
 15–17, 23, 40
seismometers, 15

tar, 7, 27–28, 29
trilobites, 18

ABOUT THE AUTHOR

Jenny Fretland VanVoorst is a writer and editor of books for young people. She enjoys learning about all kinds of topics. She lives in Minneapolis, Minnesota, with her husband, Brian, and their two pets.